DINKUM DUNNIES

DOUGLASS BAGLIN/BARBARA MULLINS

ECLIPSE BOOKS

BAGMAN'S REST Broken Hill, N.S.W.

First published in Australia 1971
by Eclipse Books
176 South Creek Road, Dee Why West, 2099
Copyright © Douglass Baglin and Barbara Mullins, 1971
Second impression May 1972
Third impression December 1972
Fourth impression June 1973
Fifth impression April 1974
Sixth impression June 1975
National Library of Australia Card
Number and ISBN 0 600 070166
Designed and produced in Australia
Printed in Singapore

DUNNIES COME IN MANY SHAPES AND SIZES

WHILE I LIVE I'LL GROW — Lumley Park, N.S.W.

LADIES — Ord River, W.A.

... AND GENTS — Cooper Creek, Qld.

AND VARIOUS ARCHITECTURAL STYLES

THE SQUAT— Historic 9-holer built by William Cox, 1830, at "Hobartville", Richmond, N.S.W.

THE LONG — Barossa Valley, S.A.

. . . AND THE SHORT
— Braidwood, N.S.W.

...AND THE TALL? — Pemberton, W.A.

THEY OCCUR IN ALL CORNERS OF THE CONTINENT

— Forrest, W.A.

— Horne Island,
Torres Strait

— Point Lookout, N.S.W.

— Utopia, N.T.

AND CATER FOR ALL CATEGORIES

CABINET LEAK
— Reptile Park, Gosford

FOR SMALL MEN WITH BIG NUGGETS
— Abandoned goldfields, Kiandra, N.S.W.

SOME ARE MATEY

TWO'S COMPANY — Wyndham, W.A.

TWO PEAS IN A POD — Balmain, N.S.W.

◄**STRICTLY FOR THE BIRDS** — Normanton, Qld.

LIVE COVERAGE — Kurnell, N.S.W.

CLASS DISTINCTION
— Brighton-le-sands, N.S.W.

SEX DISCRIMINATION
— Taronga Park Zoo, N.S.W.

— Hall's Creek, W.A.

— Pialba, Qld.

— Bilpin, N.S.W.

— South Coast, N.S.W.

AND SOME ARE UTILITARIAN

— Perth, W.A.

WIND GENERATOR
— Andamooka, S.A.

PUMPING STATION
— Kimberleys, W.A.

ROYAL FLUSH — Narrow Neck, Katoomba, N.S.W.

THE EFFLUENT SOCIETY
— Myall Lakes National Park, N.S.W.

INSIDE JOBS

HOLES-IN-THE-WALL
— Old Jail, Lyton, W.A.

NOTHING TO HIDE
— Dubbo Jail, N.S.W.

ESCAPE HATCHES
— Uralla Jail, N.S.W.

FOR ASPIRING ADMIRALS

— Cockatoo Dock, N.S.W.

AND AIR FORCE TYPES

PER ARDUA AD ASTRA ("Through straining to the stars")
— Parkes, N.S.W.

BLAST OFF!
— Arnhemland, N.T.

Could it be something I ate?
— Myall Lakes, N.S.W.

SOME COMMEMORATE THE BUSH BALLADISTS . . .

Clancy of the Overflow
—— St. Marys, N.S.W.

"The sweet-scented wattle spreads glory around
Enticing the bird and the bee . . . — Sale, Vic.

"As I lay at full rest . . . — Lord Howe Island

"In a fern-covered nest . . ." — Raymond Terrace, N.S.W.
(from Reedy Lagoon, traditional ballad)

A ROOM WITH A VIEW

— Captain Cook's Lookout, Botany Bay, N.S.W.

— Lavender Bay, N.S.W.

— Magnetic Island, Great Barrier Reef

AND EV. MOD. CON.

PANTS DRIED . . .
— Alice Springs, N.T.

WHILE YOU WAIT — Jericho, Qld.

FOR HOT PANTS?
— Min Min, Qld.

TO SUIT ALL TYPES

MILLIONAIRE'S PLAYGROUND — Great Barrier Reef, Qld.

THE DOGHOUSE — Mudgee, N.S.W. ▶

—AND SITUATIONS

— Jenolan State Forest, N.S.W.

— Andamooka opalfields, S.A.

— Glen Innes, N.S.W.

AT
YOUR CONVENIENCE

WHY BUY WHEN YOU CAN HIRE?

YOU CAN TAKE IT WITH YOU! — Public Works privy

FOR SHORT HORNS — Cattle Stud Manildra, N.S.W.

FOR THE SECURITY CONSCIOUS
— Oodnadatta, S.A

FOR LADY ELEPHANTS — Taronga Park, N.S.W.

FOR THOSE SEEKING TO IMPROVE THEMSELVES

SEAT OF LEARNING — Fisher Library, University of Sydney

BIRTHPLACE OF A NATION
— Captain Cook's Landing Place, Kurnell, N.S.W.

SIDE SHOW — Country fair, N.S.W.

FRONT STALLS

TO EACH HIS OWN — Cairns, Qld.

ANDAMOOKA, S.A.
— Where opals and men dwell underground, and only dunnies adorn the surface.

◄ORGAN GRINDER — Andamooka, S.A.

FRESH-LAID — Mackay, Qld.

IN CASE OF FLOOD — Stroud, N.S.W.

— **THEN GO** — Normanton, Qld.

GIVE GENEROUSLY — Bundaberg, Qld.

THE TWENTIETH HOLE
— Sewer outlet,
Bondi, N.S.W.